EndEx

Clive Ward

Copyright © 2017 Clive Ward/oneroofpublications.com

All rights reserved.

ISBN- 10: 1548436879
ISBN-13: 978 - 1548436872

DEDICATION

This book is dedicated to all veterans young or old.

ACKNOWLEDGMENTS

Big thanks to my wife and soul mate Elaine for her support and input. I'd also like to thank my editor Antonella Caputo for her help and advice.

CHAPTER 1

ENDEX

It's over. Your clearance chit is all signed off. You've received your last train warrant, they've taken your ID card off you at the guard room, and you walk out through the gate for the last time, it's Endex.

It doesn't matter how many years you served in the military, it will always have a lasting effect on the way you live the rest of your life. Marine, soldier, sailor or airman, whichever you may be, there are some qualities and experiences that most, if not all veterans, share.

There are 3 types of people, Civilian, Military and Veteran. Once you join the military, you can never go back to being a civilian again.

When you've left the military, you might think you are doing a great job trying to blend in to your civilian surroundings, but the signs are there, that you once served your country, sometimes without you even realising it. What you will realise is you'll never be normal again.

CIVILIAN

The word civilian relates to the 14th century French word civilien, meaning, of the civil law." The first modern usage of the word referring to non-military personnel, is thought to have been in 1829. Non-military personnel? And we all know there were lots of them about during WW2. It had to be a French word didn't it!!!

Most of the habits and traits told in this book, I have no doubt you've heard before. If you haven't, you'll find them plastered all over the internet. What I've tried to do, is collate them into categories, and add a lot of my own observations and experiences, using cartoons and stories. Yes, I might have exaggerated some of the content here and there, in fact some of it you'll find beyond exaggeration.

Hopefully, my tales will help you to spot those give away signs that you were once in the military. If you've just left, it may help you adapt to civilian life better.

You can take the man out of the military, but you can't take the military out of the man. I'm happy to be institutionalised.

10 PHRASES YOU WILL NEVER HEAR AGAIN

Stand by your beds!
The RMP is in the block.
Leave is cancelled.
Pick up the log.
Brecon
You're on stag
Breaking into double time
Open your lockers?
Contact, wait out.
Do you accept my award?

CHAPTER 2

So, you are now a civilian again, those first 30 days you'll feel great. It's a new chapter in your life, a new dawn, freedom, you've earned it. You can go to bed at a normal time, if you wake up in the middle of the night and hear it's pissing down outside, don't worry, you can happily roll over and go to sleep again. No more getting piss wet through in your sleeping bag. And better still you get to lie in. When you do eventually wake up, there won't be half a dozen other blokes in the same room.

You don't have to shave every morning, it's now a treat. Women look more feminine. You now have money left at the end of the month, and you start to find out a few new interesting facts.

Who would have thought Kiwi is not just a boot polish, it's also the name of a flightless bird native to New Zealand and a fruit! The list is endless.

KIWI POLISH

Did you know, Kiwi polish came onto the market in 1906. It was the invention of two Scotsmen who opened a boot polish factory in Melbourne, Australia in 1904. It was originally sold to farmers who used it to preserve the leather boots they wore. The polish became popular with British and American soldiers during World War One, as it helped to waterproof, their boots. The polish is also well known for its ability to produce a high shine and cover scuffs on leather shoes. So, it was Scottish Aussies who were to blame for all those wasted hours bulling my boots, when I could have been out on the piss and chasing women. Thank God, I discovered Seal, Clear and Morello, which once applied did the same job in 2 minutes.

One of the main things that stood out for me was that I didn't have to salute anybody anymore and I didn't have to cram all, of my possessions into a four foot by eight, space. Now I can sling them around where I want.

It's time to let go and grow that a huge beard and 70's sideburns, have a weird haircut or ponytail, get a few piercings. Promise yourself you'll never go to the barbers ever again, smoke some weed and get completely shit faced whenever you want! Ok that's going a bit too far. You can walk around looking like Ozzy Osborne after an all-nighter if you want, but remember, you now have, to get a job, I'm afraid.

It's time to put that CV together, so your potential new employer finds out the many, different ways you know how to kill people. Then comes the application form. Question C, 'Please include your previous addresses with dates to and from for the last 10 years'. That's it, you're fucked. You find yourself filling out paperwork for the next 10 years! You need a second or third sheet.

When you do find a job, and are due to start work on a Monday morning bright and early, you get your first flash back. That Sunday night feeling will come rushing back, shit I need to press my kit, bull my boots, iron my barrack room trousers…Chill out, you're out of the military now

CHAPTER 3

CIVILIANS IN THE WORKPLACE

You turn up to your new job at the office or where ever, freshly shaven with highly polished shoes, ironed shirt and note book and pen in your top left hand, pocket. You're ex-military. You want to create the right impression. It's to be expected of you, but believe me, you shouldn't have bothered. The fat sweaty bastard, filling his face full of crisps, sat next to you, doesn't give a shit, nor does your ponytailed new boss, who's ten years younger than you.

In the first few weeks, you work like a bastard anyway, you'll show them, you don't want to stand still. You want promotion. You want to go places. I've got news for you, you're not going anywhere, because of the years spent serving your country, you are way behind everyone else in the pecking order. But you never know you might get your bosses job eventually!

MY FIRST DAY

I remember my first job. I got a job as sand blaster at a firm that produced aero engines. From the start, I wanted to create a good impression. It wasn't long before I changed my way of thinking. I don't know what it was, but for me, from day one, I had the feeling that I was always being watched. It felt like the RSM was behind me all the time, but I found out that was just me being paranoid.

On my first day, I was shown what to do by this big intimidating Jamaican guy called Seth, my new work mate. Anyway, after 10 minutes of training he disappeared and left me with my first job. I had to blast the carbon off the surface of 180 aero engine blades, which were being reconditioned. It only took me around an hour it was easy. I even started another batch to impress Seth. When my work mate returned, he went up the wall.

'It was supposed to take you 8 hours to do those, you idiot, a whole shift,' he informed me.

And what made a bad situation even worse, I'd started on another batch of blades. They were marked for the coming weekend's overtime! There was always work stock piled on a rack, so the workers were always asked to come in on overtime on Saturday and Sunday at time and a half and double time. It was a big scam, even the gaffers were in on it!

My punishment for not toeing the line, I was given a trolley with an empty box and told to piss off. My new work mate instructed me to walk round the shop floor, and get to know my way around, and make out I was busy doing a job, until knocking off time.

KNOCKING OUT FOREIGNERS

After all, Seth had a busy afternoon, knocking out foreigners he'd bought in from outside, things friends had asked him to sand blast for them, like bike frames, car wheels and a variety of other things. When I got to know him better, I found out he was running a small business, buying old Oxford

Cambridge car wheels and parts from the scrappers or where ever, sand blasting the crap off them and exporting them to Jamaica. Back in the 80's, Oxford Cambridge parts and wheels were in demand, as they were the main make of all the taxi's.

CRACK TEST

Nobody noticed me walking round with my empty box, apart from the other half dozen workers also walking round with empty boxes.

Eventually I arrived at Crack Test, where workers sat behind a curtain checking aero engine parts for cracks, as they went zooming past on a conveyor belt. The parts had been dipped in some sort of solution, so that any cracks would show up under UV lights. I thought I'd drop by and introduce myself, and guess what, I pulled the curtain back and they were all asleep. From that day, onwards I swore I'd never travel on any airplanes using their engines ever again. Unless the flight I booked was really, cheap.

There was no RSM anymore, nobody gave a shit. Nobody went sick either, because nobody did anything, unless it was the weekend, when they could knock up time and a half or double time. Thinking about it, doing the shop floor walk reminded me of the army, walking round the barracks with a clipboard and a scrap of paper, trying to look busy until knocking off time.

OVERTIME

Time 'n' half for Saturday, or double time on a Sunday. I couldn't get enough of it. I was first to put my hand up every time. Why didn't they pay us that in the military?

I can just imagine my platoon Sergeant saying 'can I put you down for the weekend? We can pay you double and unsociable hours!'

'That's nice of you Sergeant, cheers.'

More like 'You, you and you, you're on guard duty tonight. I've booked you an early meal, get it down your face, then get your arse down the guard room! Right I need one more'. That's when you'd hide until he'd got his man. It was a bit like the kitchen scene in Jurassic Park, where the kid hides behind the cooker while being pursued by a Velociraptor. But now in

Civvy Street, it was 'I'll do it.'

After a few months of 120 hours a week, the novelty had worn off. They could shove their overtime, I wanted my life back.

GAS... GAS... GAS...

One of the main things you'll notice straight away in the workplace is that you speak a different language to your co-workers. For instance, saying Ease Springs, GAS... GAS... GAS... after a loud fart won't mean anything to them. They'll stand there amazed with your list of phrases for going to the toilet, 'Right I'm going for a shit... I'm off for a dump... or I'm off to give birth.'

When your stapler stops working, and you carry out stoppage drills, 'Stapler stops, on looking inside...' They'll think you've totally lost it!

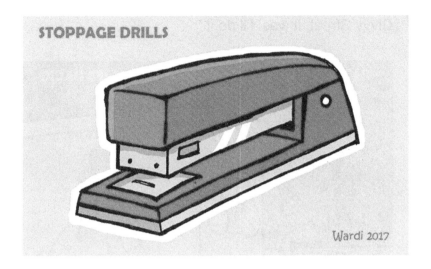

STOPPAGE DRILLS

Don't worry, they'll get used to these phrases, in fact some of them might even be adopted by them over the next few years. My advice at the beginning is to print off a military acronyms list, so your co-workers can understand you. A phonetic alphabet chart wouldn't go amiss. The last thing you want to hear in the office is S for sugar instead of Sierra and M for Mother instead of Mike, it will really annoy the shit out of you.

CIVVY PATHETIC ALPHABET

A Apple
B Bus
C Chocolate
D Donald
E Elephant
F Freddie
G Garage
H Harry
I Igloo
J Janet
K Katie
L Lollypop
M Mother
N Norman
O Octopus
P Peter
Q Queen
R Rodney
S Sugar
T Tommy
U Umbrella
V Van
W Wellington
X Xmas
Y Yarmouth
Z Zebra

Don't even bother with 'at the end of the day we've got to make sure that we are singing off the same song-sheet'. If push comes to shove we've got to be hot-to-trot from the word "go". It's a whole new ball game. We need to run a tight ship, and all that bollocks. Your co-workers will think you're nuts.

Another good bit of advice is, don't take your sense of humour too far. It could land you in trouble.

At the beginning, take it easy, a few cock jokes will be ok, but what was funny and accepted in the military, will not have the same effect at work. For instance, leaving human turds in amusing places around the workplace, won't be appreciated by your colleagues. You need to build up to something like that.

EndEx

Be warned, there's no such thing as NAAFI break. NAAFI break withdrawal, syndrome, (NBWS) is very common when you first get out. I'm sure if you have a private one to one, with your new boss and explain the situation, that you might not make it to lunch if you don't get that 30, minute break at ten o'clock, he might be sympathetic.

My boss did take pity on me and changed the break time. Now all my new civvy mates look at me mystified, when I cry "NAAFI break" loudly at 10 am every morning.

NAAFI

The Navy, Army and Air Force Institute, was created in 1920 by the British government, in order, to provide recreational facilities for the British Armed Forces, junior ranks. During WW1, canteen facilities were run by two separate companies, Expeditionary Force Canteens and

Navy and Army Canteen Board. At the end of the war, it was revealed that Expeditionary Force Canteens, had made large profits from purchases made by the troops. The public were unhappy with the situation, so in 1920, Winston Churchill, formed a committee to advise what was needed in times of war and peace by the junior ranks. NAAFI was established on the 6th December 1920 as not for profit organization and began trading in 1921.

HERE ARE A FEW MORE THINGS YOU'LL HAVE TO GET USED TO

If you've been called into the boss' office for a bollocking, don't march in, in quick time, stand to attention and await your punishment, it will freak him out and he'll call security.

You don't have to answer the phone with that pre-arranged spiel anymore. '1WFR guard room, Meanee Barracks, L/Cpl Smith speaking sir, how can I help you?'

You'll get strange looks when you ask for your brew NATO standard, or wet and warm. Then you'll find yourself trying to explain to them that 20 cups of tea a day is normal where you come from. When you do eventually get your weak gnats piss, you shouldn't have fucking bothered brew, you soon realise, it's not the same without mud, half a forestry block and a dead mozzie floating in it.

The test… If asked how you want your brew, the

answer is "Nato" - and if they understand, then they are worth talking to...

NATO STANDARD

The term NATO standard, which refers to tea/coffee with milk and two sugars, is thought to date back to the 1950's, when NATO members began trying to standardize parts for both European and American forces. But nothing will ever taste like the tea from a norgie (Norwegian container) whilst sat on the ranges all fucking day. RANGE STANDARD tastes different to any other tea, purely down to the condition of the CQMS's sock in which it is brewed.
Other abbreviations; Julie Andrews: Milk no sugar (White Nun) Whoopi Goldberg: No milk no sugar (Black Nun)

Another thing to watch out for, they'll keep asking and asking you to go on the works paint balling days. For one, all veterans hate civvies wearing combats, and the last thing you want to do is play pretend soldiers. How fucking degrading. They won't stop asking you though, my advice is give in and go. They'll never ask you again, when you take the paint balling day a bit too far. That's a point, can you fix bayonets on the paint gun, just asking?

PAINTBALLING

Paintballing began in the 1980's. The first game was played on 27 June 1981, in Henniker, New Hampshire, USA. It has become a popular pastime. For me, it's an official Walt pastime. Live Rounds or Blanks... Paint doesn't quite cut it. Mind you, I've heard it hurts like fuck when you

get hit with paint balls even through body-armour. So, respect to the Walts!!

Don't be alarmed when everybody fucks off home at 5:15 PM, and you're the only person left behind. It's probably a good thing in the early days, because your missus couldn't take the shock of seeing you before 7:00PM. And coming out in a cold sweat when you find yourself still working after lunch on a Friday is common, you'll get used to it.

CHAPTER 4

U TURN

There are lots of stories of guys joining straight back up again after they'd left, but for me it was the best day of my life, or so I thought. That wore off quickly, when I realised the grass is not greener on the other side. I couldn't believe it. It suddenly dawned on me I was in this boring 9 to 5 clock-watching job. It wasn't long before I found myself missing the military. Daydreaming of tabbing it across a training area, that smell of hexi-blocks, cordite, Kiwi, scrim net, linseed oil and waking up soaked in my basha. Thinking about the thunder flash in the back of a 4 tonner, hot brass down my neck, filling my beret with empty cases, cleaning mess tins, a brew on exercise. The sense of humour on tour or on exercise; then having a laugh about it afterwards, getting shit faced down the NAAFI. All those memories brought a smile to my face. I would sooner be bored shitless in the butts all day than the shit job I found myself in.

I had a mate who couldn't wait to leave, he'd serve 6 years. Before the year was out, he'd joined back up again. He couldn't handle Civvy Street and struggled to find the right job. Eventually when he did find a job, it was at a company that produced balloons. This was in the 70's, so it was manual testing before they bagged them up. Poor bloke spent everyday testing balloons, which involved picking up said balloon, stretching it twice, then placing the balloon on the airflow, so it inflates at least 3 inches in diameter, then letting the air out so it made that fart noise. The guy did this for 60 hours a week for a month, it sent him nuts. He was soon back in the army.

Another guy, who I can't name for legal reasons, also had trouble finding the right job. He ended up working in a large shop selling motor bikes. From day one he couldn't get on with the sales manager. After working there for a while, he heard from one of his work colleagues that they were going to get rid of him later that afternoon. So, he decided in typical squaddie fashion that he would have the last laugh. Before he went off for his 30, minute dinner break, he decided to attach a bike inner tube tight to the air flow with gaffer tape and leave. About 5 minutes later BOOM! The windows in the shop blew out causing loads of damage and panic. It was like being on the Falls road again. He didn't join up again, instead he ended up being detained at Her Majesty's pleasure.

Yes, leaving the military too early can be a big mistake for some. You'll be adding your old military mates on Facebook and crying into a tin of beer in no time. The grass isn't always greener in Civvy Street, but at least you won't get your head ripped off by the RSM when you walk on it!

So, you've been out for few months now and your new civvy mates are doing your head in. It is really, important to find another veteran friend before you start to go insane. Don't worry, you'll be able to spot a fellow veteran a mile away.

For instance, if you are walking down the street minding your own business, looking all around, the fucking non- existent enemies aren't getting you from behind. Suddenly, a, car back fires. You see a random person dive for cover in a shop doorway and assume the prone position. You watch as he scans roof tops for the enemy, then grasps his umbrella like a rifle, fumbles in his coat pockets for a 'magazine of 30. Then much to your surprise, you find yourself lying next to him. You know straight away this person is a veteran. Finding new friends with the same mental disorder as you, is, important. After laughing the incident off as a false alarm and getting strange looks from passers-by, you stand up dust yourselves down, then stamp your feet as though you're trying to get your lightweights hanging right, but you're not wearing light weights anymore.

You now have a new veteran friend. To seal your new friendship, you head for the nearest pub or bar for a beer and a pull up a sandbag session. Walking to the pub, you find you both move off with your left foot first, moving quickly as though you're worried the cookhouse is closing any minute, and often find yourself trying to get in step with your new friend. This is all normal, don't worry, as long, as you don't swing your arms, you'll look a right twat if you do.

CHAPTER 5

CIVILIANS

A shit day in the military is a shit day with mates. A good day in Civvy Street doesn't even come close to being as good as a shit day in the military. Yes, you'll soon make civilian friends when you're out the military, but they'll never properly understand you and you'll never properly understand them. What is noticeable straight away is most of them talk shit. My usual response is;

'I see that you are fluent in Gibbering Moronese. unfortunately, I'm not.'

'You generate more waffle than the waffle making machine in a waffle factory.'

'You are about as entertaining as watching grass grow in a window box, fuckoff.'

When they find out you are ex-military your civilian friends will tell you why they couldn't join up. They will also ask the most stupid and inappropriate questions like,

'You were in the military, really? You don't look old enough!'

'Have you ever shot anyone?'

'I would have joined up myself, but the doctor told me I had flat feet.'

Or 'I failed the eye test.' How many fucking times have we heard that!

'What's the worst thing that happened to you over there?'

'Did you go to Afghanistan? It's, ok I know you can't talk about it, I can't imagine some of the stuff you've done.'

Getting used to listening to comments like that and the stupid questions, will take a while. If you feel it carries on for too long, you are legally within your rights to take one or two of them to one side and threaten to strangle them. That will do the trick, I'm sure the stupid questions will subside.

It's no good sparking up a serious conversation and telling them your stories, civvies won't understand what you're talking about when you start getting technical, and most civvies think integrity is something by Calvin Klein.

Forget jokes. All your jokes will make civvies want to literally vomit or take massive offence. Back in the military it was the 'norm' to tell your mates 'Right lads, I'm off for a wank,' they didn't bat an eye lid. Say that to a civvy and they would go into fucking shock and have a panic attack. 'You can't say that, you can't say that!'

CINEMA

You know you're a veteran when you shout at the screen, 'That's bollocks... 300 rounds from a 30, round magazine, do me a fucking favour.'

Not the best idea when you're in a packed cinema. Come on! Seeing Arnold Schwarzenegger reload his Uzi in a movie, is about as rare as rocking horse shit. Don't you just hate it when they take cover behind plywood and then shoot at the radiator and the fucking car explodes?

Or do you prefer the quiet approach? You count rounds expended during a battle scene and then lean over and whisper in the missus's ear, 'When's he going to change his fucking magazine?' then get a sharp nudge in your side for your troubles, which makes you spill your popcorn all over the place. As if your missus is really interested in the comment.

TV

Meanwhile, watching TV at home can be just as frustrating for a veteran, especially when you've just bought a new one. Every year TV's get more and more complicated.

You know how to break down and reassemble your weapon in the dark, but can you fuck set up your new TV with the remote. That's if you can find the bloody thing after the kids have hidden it, or the dog's decided it's his new toy. Then once you've worked out how it works, or the missus has, you now have to compete with three other TVs around the house, blaring out shit pop music, which the kids sing along to, then the bloody missus joins in. It makes you want to slit your wrists.

Finally, the kids are all tucked up in bed. Now it's time to get revenge on your missus. You've discovered the pause button, brilliant, so now you can pause the war movie you're both watching, to inspect the characters in uniform.

  'You see those buttons, they're the wrong type, and his boots are bogging,' you'll inform her.
  'Ok, you've made your point. Can we carry on watching the film please?' she'll answer, with a resigned look on her face.

Or are you one of those who can't watch a war movie without giving a running commentary? 'That's a T62 fume extractor two thirds along the barrel, gaps between the third and fourth and the fourth and fifth road wheel.'

While I'm on the subject, of war movies, what's the betting the film Zulu is in your DVD collection. I bet you can recite most of the script because you've watched it with your buddies dozens of times while on guard duty or standby, or bored out your tree waiting for nothing to happen.

'Don't throw those bloody spears at me,' that famous line from the movie is quoted by a veteran every day somewhere on the planet. Not a lot of people know this, but Michael Caine never actually said that in the movie. The movie was pure class though, and still is. I can hear you all singing Men of Harlech now... *Men of Harlech stop your dreaming, can't you see their spear points gleaming...* The film Zulu was released in 1964 and is still regularly shown on TV.

I know for a fact, that Sir Michael was a Lt at Rorke's Drift, and, also commanded an Irish Guards Battalion in Operation Market Garden, then he became a spy in the 60's after which he began driving mini's and robbing banks.

SIR MICHAEL CAINE

Born in 1933 in Rotherhithe, London. Maurice Joseph Micklewhite Jr took on the stage name Michael Caine. He did two years National Service from 1952 to 1954, (National Service, virtually anyone who didn't have flat feet or VD did their bit) serving with the Royal Fusiliers in Iserlohn, Germany and on active service during the Korean War. He is a keen supporter of bringing back National Service.

AND HERE ARE A FEW MORE 'CELEBRITIES' WHO DID THEIR BIT FOR QUEEN AND COUNTRY.

David Niven – Highland Light Infantry
Bill Roache – Royal Welsh Fusiliers
Michael Parkinson – Royal Army Pay Corp
Nigel Benn – Royal Regiment of Fusiliers
Alec Guiness – Royal Navy
Donald Pleasence - RAF
Dirk Bogarde – Royal Corp of Signals and Queen's Royal Regiment
Sean Connery - Royal Navy
Richard Burton - Royal Air Force
Anthony Quayle – Special Ops
Sir Dickie Attenborough – Royal Air Force
George Cole (Arthur Daley) - Royal Air Force
Dennis Healey – Royal Engineers
Leslie Grantham aka 'Dirty Den' - Royal Fusiliers
Bernard Cribbins – Parachute Regiment
Frank Carson – Parachute Regiment
Murray Walker – Royal Armoured Corp and Royal Scots Greys
Paddy Ashdown (ex Lib Dem) - Royal Marines

Personally, I'm sick of TV. We've gone from 2 channels in the 60's to being able to tune into any channel in the world. All I find myself doing now is watching the news channels, Sky or CNN on a loop, and constantly moaning that there's nothing decent to watch anymore. But what pisses me off most of all and I think most veterans will agree, are these reality TV shows, Big Brother, I'm a Celebrity and Survival shows, when you see people turning on the water works after 2 weeks of not seeing their families, and then they get letters from home. Give me a break! It makes you want to throw a brick at the TV screen.

CHAPTER 6

WALT'S AND WANKERS

We've all seen the Walt's being exposed in the media, marching along on Remembrance Day, dressed to the 9's, in their SAS berets, wearing dozens of medals they're not entitled to. Some of them give themselves away from the minute they appear, when they show up wearing that many gongs, they put every South American dictator to shame.

The ones I really hate, are those pretending to be veterans so they can line their own pockets. The ones standing outside supermarkets and on the local markets selling poppy badges, pretending to collect money for military charities. They need a good kicking and need locking up, on a wing full of real ex-military, who have gone off the rails.

I only had one experience with a Walt. Well, I wouldn't even give him the dignity of calling him a Walt, more like a wanker. He lived on our estate, he was about 30 and looked a bit of a twat. Every time I saw him, he'd be wearing full combats with an air rifle strapped over his shoulder, and half a dozen chavs and slobbering teenage girls following him around, which started to raise alarm bells with the locals.

Was he a Walt? Absolutely nothing wrong with wearing combats and carrying an air rifle. You could say it was a bit OTT, Walter McWalty, maybe he was doing a bit of beating or pheasant slaughtering. Then I found out from my son, that this guy was telling all the kids he'd been in the Special Forces. Telling them porkies about being in Belfast and the Falklands, etc.

One evening my son's 12, year old mate came around. I noticed he had a right shiner, so I asked him who did it.

'It was ******' he said. This wanker had told him, that no "niggers" were, allowed to walk down 'HIS' street.
    'Did he now? Come on follow me,' I said, heading towards the front door.

I was soon face to face with the scumbag, but I didn't have to do a thing. His mother, who I thought was there to back him up, smacked him around the head with a wooden fence post. It was hilarious.

'Get in that bloody house you!' He never said a word. He just ran indoors, screaming with pain. I was even more surprised, when his mother apologised for his behaviour. After that, apart from a few all night vigils to make sure my car didn't get vandalized, we didn't see him again.

Two years later, I read in the paper he had been sent down for shooting and blinding a local drug dealer in a telephone box. What became of him after that I haven't got a clue. He's probably a fully, grown Walt now.

When that time of year comes around for maximum Walt activity, if you do spot or suspect a Walt, post their likely location, they all need outing.

CHAPTER 7

CHRISTMAS

After all those years serving your country, you can now experience Christmas at home with your family and friends. You've decorated your Christmas tree with chemical lights (Tactical) and Engineer tape, and placed the Christmas presents around the tree. Then the Missus asks. 'Have you prepared for Santa coming?'

'Yes, there are trip wires on all points of entry, including the chimney of course. The lazer beam defence system is on and primed, the alarms are on, booby traps set. Oh, and the nerve gas canisters are set and are all fully functional, the satellite tracking system is...'

'I was thinking more of a mince pie and glass of sherry you idiot.'

Christmas morning, time to open the presents. But it's not the shoe box size you used to get when you were on deployment, full of goodies, cigarettes, cakes, biscuits, sweets and porn. Now it's a can of Lynx spray and shampoo from your Gran, a pair of socks from the kids, a hand knitted military style Christmas jumper from the missus, because she wants you to look a prize prick, when the in-laws turn up.

CHRISTMAS MORNING, TIME TO OPEN THE PRESENTS

You're all sitting down for Christmas dinner, you give the command, "fix bayonets," and everyone tucks in. You've finished your dinner before everyone else has had chance to eat their first Brussel sprout. Then it's time to relax in front of that new TV to watch, you've guessed it, fucking Zulu again, followed by Von Ryan's express.

"TARGETS TO YOUR FRONT GO ON!"

Alternatively, if you're lucky enough, you might get a sprinkling of snow. If you do, it's out in the garden for the annual snowball fight against the in-laws, who start to look at you with a blank stare. You find yourself automatically giving out fire control orders to your kids, who do a quick right flanking, while you pound them with snow ball after snow ball, making sure nearly all of them are head shots, until your kids arrive for the kill.

ANNUAL SNOWBALL FIGHT AGAINST THE IN-LAWS

Now Christmas is over for another year and you're busy (de-camming), pulling down the Christmas decorations, and putting them back in the shed or garage, that's when you spot your old Bergen and you can't help having a good old sniff for old time's sake. That smell... it's like you never left. A mixture of pine forest, smoke and dirt.   And it's not long before those memories start flooding back. Weeks of tabbing for miles, freezing your nuts off on active duty in some far forgotten land, or on exercise. Delving deeper into the Bergen, you find an old tube of cam cream, and a pair of old green socks, that should have been taken out and shot years ago. The ultimate Christmas present, a packet of hard tac biscuits and a tin of cheese possessed. Now it really is Christmas.

HIDDEN TREASURE...

Wardi 2017

HARD TACK BISCUITS

Long lasting biscuits have been around in various forms since ancient Egyptian times. Tack was a word used by British sailors to refer to food. Early sailors would dunk their biscuits in liquid to soften them. For long voyages the biscuits were baked four times to make them harder and longer lasting. Spare a thought for the British Navy of 1588, whose daily rations were one pound of biscuits and a gallon of beer.

6 THINGS YOU DID IN THE MILITARY THAT WILL GET YOU IN TROUBLE OR ARRESTED ON CIVVY STREET

1. Drive your vehicle straight through a field full of crops, then demolish the side of a barn without a care in the world

2. Jump on the bar at your local, pull your trousers down, shove a newspaper up your arse and light it up, and do the dance of the flaming arseholes
3. Blowing up a bridge
4. Piss out of the back of a moving truck
5. Invade your Islamic neighbour, after receiving information they could be hoarding weapons of mass destruction.
6. Draw a penis on the face of a work colleague who is taking a crafty nap, then wake him up and tell him that the Boss is looking for him.

CHAPTER 8

BEDTIME

Now you're a veteran, you can go to bed in the knowledge you'll never be woken up in the middle of the night again, for that dreaded 2 till 4 stag or watch. Unless you sleep walk like me, and go for a wander and wake up outside in the garden checking your perimeter fencing. Or after a night on the piss, you get out of bed still pissed out of your face and take a piss in what you think is the next soldier's locker, and get the shock of your life when your missus yells, 'what the hell do you think you're doing? Not again for fuck's sake!' Suddenly you realise you've just pissed all over her clothes, on her side of the wardrobe.

Don't worry these habits will leave you at some stage, and you'll be able to navigate yourself to the bog easily, you'll even get there with your shooting eye shut, to preserve your night vision.

It's funny. Even after all these years out of the military, before I go to sleep I find myself physically looking for my weapon, then suddenly realise I don't have to do that anymore. Sometimes I look towards my bay windows looking for the best firing position, just in case something happens in the street during the night. Or is that just me.

It's Saturday morning, it's time for the missus to get her own back, when she shouts, 'STAND—TO' down your lughole, because it's the only way she can get you up on a Saturday morning. The main reasons you don't want to get up is one, it's Saturday, and two, she wants you to take her shopping.

When you do eventually prise yourself out of bed around mid-morning, still half asleep, you slouch downstairs and head for the front door, open it and stand there, stark bollock naked, scratching your arse, yawning away, wondering why the old couple over the road are giving you funny looks. 'Look Alfred it's him again!' Then you realise you are no longer in the military.

Long gone are the days when you were lying in your maggot, staring out over the training area at some distant house lights, wishing you were tucked up in bed. Well, now you are that person tucked up in bed.

But sometimes, don't you wish you were back out there again with your old buddies?

SHOPPING

Is there anything worse than being dragged to the shops for hours? Going shopping for a veteran means 'GET IN, BUY WHAT YOU NEED AND GET THE FUCK OUT OF THERE.' We go shopping to buy what we want. Women go shopping to find what they want. The missus to a T. 'I went to buy a dress, but I saw a beautiful pair of shoes, so I bought this handbag.'

I just want to get it over with as quickly as possible, but I know that isn't going to happen. When it comes to getting ready, within 5 minutes, I'm waiting in the car with the engine running, while the missus is prancing around getting ready. I've used half a tank of fuel by the time she appears.

Once we arrive in town, we park up, there's no time to waste, let's get it done. Veterans walk fast everywhere, we're physically incapable of walking at the shopping pace. You might be doing a great job blending into your civilian surroundings, but your walk is always going to give you away. Veterans walk with a purpose, as if their trip to the shops is like you're late for guard duty. I get about 5 yards ahead of the missus and...

'Will you slow down? it's not a race, you're not in the army now you know.' Then comes the emotional blackmail. 'I'll tell you what, why don't you piss off home, I'll catch the bus!' I slow down and let her catch up.

We approach the first shop and enter. It's a clothing shop. I start to walk in straight lines, trying not to spend a minute longer in there than necessary, but it's physically impossible for my missus to do that, she's all over the place. Veterans can walk around the streets of Belfast patrolling for hours, but put them in a shop and they're fucked. They lack the energy and endurance a woman has and the women seem to know where everything is.

MISSION SHREDDIES

Suddenly I realise I need some new underwear. It could take ages to track them down. Then I spot a young female assistant in the distance.

'Excuse me young lady, could you tell me where I

can find some shreddies?' She looked confused.
'Kecks, grundies, skids? You know shreddies,' I said.

She gives me that blank stare, she hasn't got a clue what I'm on about and then she says, 'Sorry, we don't sell breakfast cereal, this is a clothing store.'

I give up all hope of purchasing the shreddies and start to panic. My missus has been missing for a while now. The only way to locate her, is to give her a call on my mobile phone.

'Where are you over?'
'I'm in the handbag aisle, where are you?'
'Long story, your location figures two... over.'
'Tango, Whiskey, Alpha, Tango... out.'

I soon located her in the distance, luckily my wife fully understands hand signals, especially the 'On Me' signal when out shopping. I have her well trained, or should that be she has me well trained.

From now on, it's buddy- buddy, as she helps me find my shreddies and we both head for the check out. Me with my new shreddies, her with her new yellow handbag! Shit "YELLOW HANDBAG," instant flash back of Wolfgang, Soltau 1982!

'Will you stop day dreaming and get your money out.'

I pay for the goods and we leave, to head for the supermarket before END EX. More of the same I'm afraid. I stand back amazed, observing my wife spend an age deciding which type of salt she wants to buy. Eventually we make it to the check-out and start to load the food on the conveyer belt, then I hear...'Would you like help with your packing, dear?'

So how is it, after spending all those years in the military, someone now wants to help me pack my gear?

'No thanks, I'll manage. I was in the military, you know!'

Then comes her sarcastic chuckle, because she's heard the same comment at least ten times that day. Now it's a competition. She starts to race the food items through the till, in the hope of embarrassing me, but she's got no chance. Freezer food in freezer bag, fridge food - and beer- in a second, cupboard food in a third bag. It's like packing to go on exercise.... All sorted.

Avoiding the Polish car cleaners, we head back to the car. It's the other half's turn now, she's way ahead, it's payback time.

'What's the rush?' I say, 'Hold on, I just need to pop into Millets.'

Let's face it, you can't walk past Millets or any other camping shop, without going in to buy a new bit of kit, even though you'll never actually use it.

At last we arrive home. I park the car and head into the house, carrying all 12 bags of shopping with my left hand.

CHAPTER 9

BIRTHDAYS

I love birthdays. You know you're a veteran, and so does everyone else when you arrive at one of your kid's friends, birthday parties and your kids look like commandos, after you spent hours painting their faces with that army issue camouflage, black and green face paint, you found in the garage at Christmas, expiry date 12.07.1982.

Every other parent drops their kids off. You can't do that, you have, to hang around, because your kids are army brats, and if a civvy brat threatens them, they'll kick off. Plus, when they've eaten most of their host's party food, you are at the ready. Those years and years of spending time at parties around the married quarters come into action for when your brats throw up. You're ready to catch it mid-flight like an England wicket keeper. Years and years of practice has prepared you for that moment. The other parents stand back in awe, but if someone else's brat throws up, you laugh and find it hilarious.

What really makes me laugh and proud, though, is when your brat has had enough and turns to you and says, 'can we go home now? I'm chin strapped!'

EATING OUT AND MEALTIMES

Why is it people can't understand why veterans eat so ridiculously fast, like it's going to be taken away any minute? I eat like a vacuum cleaner. I can eat an entire large pizza in 5 minutes. Remember, they don't have a clue that in the military to appreciate your food was a rarity. When you've licked your spoon, clean and put it back in you breast pocket and everybody is sitting back having enjoyed their meal, you sound off with that typical military belch of appreciation, opening your mouth wide enough to reach the required decibels.

'Did you have to do that? I can't take you anywhere,' the missus will say.

Fast food to me means exactly that, get in get out. I drive through every time now. We used to eat in, but the wife and kids take ages. I've eaten my 5 burgers and fries in 5 minutes, flat. My wife eats at a snail's pace, it drives me nuts. I don't understand why you can't have the next burger unwrapped and ready to go before you've finished the last. Not moving with a purpose is absolutely mind boggling!

And what's all this expiry date crap? I'd never heard of it until I was out. There was no such thing as sell by or expiry date on food, if it smelt fine, you just ate it.

You know you're a veteran when you give the missus a day off and decide to become head-chef for the day. Then you fuck it up, now it's Range Stew for dinner.

Does anybody get Compo Withdrawal Syndrome when they look in the cupboard and there's nothing to eat? I remember back in Germany when wages were crap, we'd often run out of food, that's when we got the real grub out. The kids didn't have a clue. The other advantage was none of us had a shit for a week, so we saved a fortune on bog roll and nappies.

You know you're a veteran when you notice no one shouts, 'one fucking sausage' when you're at a motorway service station, helping yourself to breakfast, and when you ask where the diggers or gobbling rods are instead of cutlery, they haven't got a clue what you're talking about.

STEALING, OR SHOULD I SAY ACQUIRING

In the military, if you got caught stealing money or personal stuff like jewellery, it could be career ending. That was it, you were labelled as a thief. But stealing, or acquiring missing issued kit, was different. It was just seen as getting your kit back. For instance, if you put your PT shirt in the drying room alongside everyone else's and went back the next day and there was only one shirt left, then it was yours. Even though it was a different colour and you could only just squeeze into it. Soldiers will hoard and acquire all sorts of stuff whether they needed it or not.

Now I'm in Civvy Street, I still do that, but now I've taken it a stage further. I feel the need to acquire things that will be of no fucking use whatsoever.

Recently, I arrived home from work with a new piece of furniture for the house.

'Look what I picked up from work, a bog seat. Someone had just thrown it into the skip, it's nearly brand new.'
'Great, put it with the other 3 in the shed,' the wife sighed.

I didn't need it, but I just had to have it. Masking tape, marker pens and torch batteries are my favourite items.

SWEAR LIKE A TROOPER

The term dates back, to the 1700's and refers to British Cavalry Troopers who were uneducated and used bad language all the time.

Swearing in front of people constantly, I know I shouldn't but I can't, fucking help it. I never swore once before I joined up. Now I'm a veteran I'm even worse, especially at home. For example, "for fucks sake, this bastard washing machine's tits-up again." What I really meant to say was, "darling this Hoover Dynamic DXCC69W3 9kg washing machine is broken, it may require servicing." I've tried to cut down my swearing. One day at a time that's what I say. I've now limited myself to 4-fucks, 3-Bastards and 5-shit's a day. I've completely eradicated the C word, but the number of fucks does vary, depending on my proximity to the wife.

DIY

It doesn't matter what you did in the military you are an expert in DIY. Black masking tape can fix anything! You used to find a roll of black nasty in every drawer in the house. Now that you're out, you'll probably still find some in your organized G1098, "it's not corrugated iron, it's wriggly tin," shed or garage. You'll usually find it next to your emergency crate of beer and your, still working, 20yr old compo can opener, green string, torch batteries and paracord.

My son was in the Navy. When he comes around, he always asks me if he can borrow a bit of kit. I make him sign a 1033 every time, I don't trust those, matelots. That reminds me, he's still got 2 of my Jerry-cans.

GARDENING?

You just can't do it, can you. Go on, step on that grass. You throw caution to the wind, it feels wrong, doesn't it? You never walked on the grass back in the military, because there was always an NCO hiding somewhere nearby. No matter where you were, what time it was, or what else was going on, 9 times out of 10 you'd get caught, and the next thing you'd hear was, 'GET THE FUCK OFF MY GRASS, YOU

WORTHLESS PIECE OF SHIT. YES, YOU!' Not anymore, you just stand there, waiting for someone to yell at you, but nobody comes. Then you yell 'WHERE THE FUCK ARE YOU NOW SERGEANT MAJOR?'

For the first time, you have a garden to look after. Your own bit of turf, your little bit of training area. The wife is imagining a nice lawn, a little bird table perhaps, a veggie patch, flower beds and a barbeque area. But you're thinking, I could dig a sniper hide, just behind that front hedge, to intercept the postman. Then over a cuppa, sitting on the patio, you let it slip.

'This front lawn would look amazing with a machine gun position in the corner. I'm an expert at digging holes, so it shouldn't be a problem darling.'

Then you get up and start to remove the lower branches from the trees, with your one metre machete, to clear your field of fire, 'That should do the trick.'

Now she wants a washing line, put up…No problem, her washing line will be the best in the neighbourhood, because it's Para-cord, secured with a quick release jungle knot. While she pegs out the washing on her unbreakable, drooping, useless washing line, you and the kids are busy digging a two man, trench with sleeping bay on the front lawn.

CHAPTER 10

PERSONAL HYGIENE

Remember waking up in the morning, in the same room with dozens of blokes getting out of their pits and heading for the washroom, for a shit, shower and shave at the same time. Sometimes you even had to queue… yep, nothing's changed in our house, I'm always last in the queue. But at least now, when I do eventually get to have a wash, there's nobody in the cubicle behind me knocking one out, over a sticky, handed around copy of Readers Wives, while I'm trying to brush my teeth.

Talking of knocking one out. Why is it now every time I see a Porta-loo, I get the urge to knock one out for old times' sake, whether it's in town or at a building site. It gets awkward at music festivals, with the long queues, but that's just how it goes, I enjoy a challenge. Is it just me or do any other veterans out there have the same problem? I have, to draw penises in every bog I've ever took a shit in. Those days are over, but some habits are hard to shake off. Like wearing flip-flops in a shower, no matter where you are.

FLIP FLOPS

The modern flip flop originates from Japan and was popular with US service personnel, who took them back to America after WW2. Various forms of the flip flop have been worn since 1500BC, when they were worn by ancient Egyptians.

CLEANING

The wife hates it when I give her a hand with the cleaning. She always complains she can never find anything after I've reorganised the cupboards.

When you've hired a caravan for week in Skegness, the last day is spent scrubbing it out for handover (Marching out) as if it's an Army Quarter. If anyone owns a static caravan for hire and it's in shit state, just find an ex pad to hire it to, they'll soon have it spotlessly clean. When we did eventually escape from the caravan, about 20 miles out of Skegness, she said, 'Shit, I forgot to clean the grill on the cooker, we'll have to go back.' We haven't hired a caravan since.

I've heard nowadays when it comes to handing your army quarter over, you are, allowed to hire a private cleaning company to do it for you. You just do a surface clean, hoover and then leave it to them. That's cheating!

DISCIPLINE

Once I'd been out of the military a while. I tried a little army discipline on my 15, year old daughter, after she left the bathroom in shite state.

'Listen in young lady,' I requested in a firm voice. 'This bog is gopping, you've got approximately one hour to sort it out,' I said pointing at my G10, never broken, run late or let me down watch. 'When I get back, it had better be fucking right.'

'Oh dad, stop being an idiot, you left the army years ago... Oh, by the way, is it still ok for me to go in to town tonight?'

'Yes, I suppose so.'

PHRASES

I find myself still using the following phrases, does anyone else? I'm not going to translate, if you're a civvy reading this, sorry.

Say seen when seen
Mag to grid
Well done that man
buckshee
Say again
dark hours
At the end of the day

Dhobi
Dhobi dust
Outside areas picking up the local youths Stella can
Wait one
Crack on
Say again
Figures...
On!' to cease movements or manoeuvring.
Stand by
Prepare to move...Move
stand down
Block jobs
actions on
Diggers
Scoff
Rug rats
Bills (underwear)
Sorted
Muppet
Locker
Wagon
No Dramas
Bog standard
Down range
Spunk trench

CHAVCO

When I served, we used Mapco and then Bapco and they both baffled the shit out of me. A great read though, for dyslexics on stag! But I'm totally lost when it comes to the CHAVCO that Civvies use e.g. "I swear down," "I'll bang you out," what the fuck does that mean?

DOCTOR

You know you're a veteran when you find out being able to see a doctor or a dentist when you want, is no longer an option. It isn't going to happen anymore. Now you have, to book an appointment, sometimes 2 or 3 weeks in advance to see a doctor. But at least if you get a snotty nose in Civvy Street, you'll be rewarded with a few days off work. Go sick in the military and it was, 'take these ibuprofen and soldier on.' Or if you were lucky, and you were really, ill, you'd be given a 2 day, sick chit. Which meant "light duties."

Light duties my arse! You still had to work. Either you got shoved on fatigues or you were stuck out in the middle of nowhere in the pouring rain, being used as a marker for the CO's Friday afternoon cross-country.

DENTIST

I used to dread going to the military dentist, back in the day. I still dread going today. It's not the pain or the size of the needle, it's the size of the fucking bill you get slapped with.

CHAPTER 11

HOLIDAYS

You know you're a veteran when you still say, "pack kit," when going on holiday. All the places you've previously visited are, or were, trouble spots and war zones, or places where you can get frostbitten and suntanned in the same week.

Now it's time for a proper holiday, what you used to call leave or R&R, only now you're not told when to take it, you can take it when you want in most jobs. So where are you going to go? The family want to go camping. You say no way, the last thing you want to do is to go camping when you've already spent enough time in that environment to last a lifetime. But they keep persisting, so you tell them, 'Ok, as, long as we can go with no tent or sleeping bags.' In the end you give in, but you want to show them what real camping is about, so you take the family camping to the local zoo's reptile house, using hammocks.

You might have slept in the shittiest places on earth, drank tea with forestry blocks floating in it, and eaten cold compo for weeks. But why is it now you're out, you won't book a hotel holiday unless it's got a 4 or 5, star rating with a fully stocked mini-bar and a dog's bollocks restaurant. You hate flight delays. That might have something to do with monging around in hangers at Brize Norton for hours, waiting for that crab air flight to some sweaty shit hole.

THE GERMAN

It's a well-known fact that the Germans are famous for getting up early to secure their sun loungers with a towel, some even go to the trouble of using towels imprinted with a Union Jack! The sneaky fokers. They're Germans that's what they do. They might have won the beach towel war, we'll allow them to win that battle, oh and a couple of world cups, but they'll always be reminded who won the two world wars.

It's all friendly banter though. What really upsets a vet, especially "a vet that has done his time stationed in Germany protecting them from the pending red army invasion," is when they sit at the bar in the evening after winning the battle of the sun-loungers and hogging the pool. They slag us Brits off in German, and think us Brits can't understand them.

That's going a bit too far.

They get the shock of their lives, when suddenly, you butt into their conversation using fluent German you picked up after watching that stupid parrot on BFBS TV at 1830, teaching us all basic German, Monday to Friday every week.

I knew it would have its uses one day. *'Entschuldigen Sie bitte, was hast du gesagt du, Wichser?'* (Excuse me please, what did you say you wanker.) Lost for words, their faces start to turn red, then they spend the rest of the night apologising.

On the plus side, suddenly your holiday package changes from B&B to all-inclusive, as they buy you drinks for the rest of the week.

Just to let you know by the way, after many surveys, it's a fact that Germans think us Brits hog the sun loungers too. German is one of the hardest languages to learn, probably explains why most of us cold war veterans didn't get beyond Basic German.

CAR

After you've first paraded the motor and checked for devices, you give the order prepare to move to the missus.

You know you're a veteran when you're driving down country lanes and surveying the open ground. You say to the missus, who is busy trying to read the European 1979 AA map that you kept from when you were stationed in Germany, along with your now useless BFG petrol coupons.

 'Good tank country this. I could get a whole platoon in that forestry block.'

After giving you that long suffering resigned look, she'll reply, 'Will you just shut up and drive.'
'The large oak tree to our left will be known as "Tree," the small building to our left will be known as "Barn." It never leaves you, you know.

'I could get a whole platoon in that forestry block'

The satnav your old man bought you years ago, is still in its box in the boot, never been used. 'You can't beat a map,' you say when your missus moans about getting lost. Sorry, but tapping a postcode into a machine takes the fun out of a day out, unless you're trying to find a pub of course. What's wrong with getting lost now and again? Ask my ex Platoon Commander, he couldn't read a map if it was tattooed to his eye lids. Getting lost in Germany meant barn for the night, beer, sausages and the farmer's daughter... may be.

'How long do you think it will take us to get there?' the missus asks.

You give her the ETA and you're bang on, and that's even with you setting your G1098 watch five minutes fast for any emergencies, but you have the missus doing revised ETA's just in case you need to speed up or slow down... it's a military thing.

One hour later, after getting lost several times, you arrive at your old barracks and find it's been turned into a holding camp for failed asylum seekers. Most of the barracks you served in have long since been demolished. You have a sad moment remembering the good old days, but little sympathy from the missus, who utters the words, 'you see, I bloody told you it would be a wasted journey, can we go home now?'

On the way back, you switch driving duties and you fall asleep within five minutes. In fact, you fall asleep in any vehicle if you are not driving. I wonder where you picked that habit up from?

AA ROAD MAP

The AA came into existence in 1905, when a group of drivers got together to warn other motorists about speed traps. AA routes were introduced in 1910.

A TRIP TO LONDON

Going on day trips can be great fun, until you walk into the Imperial War Museum and the first thing you see is a mannequin wearing the same uniform that you were issued with when you joined up. Then you head for the Tower of London and find out the Beefeaters are all younger than you are. Later walking down, the Mall you see some Chelsea Pensioners, that's when you recognise your old RSM.

CHAPTER 12

BONFIRE NIGHT

After a few years, I'd had enough of sand blasting engine parts to last me a life time, so I started my own business, and was quite successful.

I'd produced a magazine called Smut, a sort of poor man's Viz comic. They created the market place, so me and my business partner, jumped on the band wagon and we made a right killing for a while, before Loaded and Nuts appeared on the scene.

So, come bonfire night, me and my crazy ex-squaddie business partner decided to show off and spend our hard, earned cash on fireworks. We didn't want any old shitty corner shop fireworks, we wanted the bollocks. We're talking London New Year's Eve Armageddon fireworks. After all we were veterans, we knew all about big bangs, or so we thought.

Determined we wanted the best firework display ever, we started to prepare, you could say we had money to burn. The problem was location. We lived on a council estate. Our gardens were too small. The decision was made, my business partner's brother-in-law, had the biggest garden, about 10 by 8 yards. We persuaded him to hold the party there. He had no idea what he'd let himself in for. The word had got out, the SMUT lads were holding a firework display.

We'd spent over a grand on dodgy Chinese display fireworks. Most of what we bought were pretty big, a lot bigger than your standard firework. There were two fireworks in the box that stood out, they were massive, both the size of 3 foot drain pipes. Oh well, they must be safe or they wouldn't have sold them to us. It was a clear night, perfect for a council estate bonfire party. There were people all over the place, on sheds, garages, up trees, trying to catch the best view. 'They wouldn't be disappointed!'

Our families had the best seats. Around 20 of us were standing or sitting in the garden, in front of the patio doors, busy drinking beer and ramming hot dogs down our throats, waiting for the spectacle to begin. At first it was great, but nothing spectacular, then it was time to let the two big ones go. We decided to light them at the same time, hoping to get them out the way quickly.

From the moment, we lit the touch paper... *KA-BOOM!* All hell broke loose, these two fireworks were 80 x repeater display fireworks. I found this out later. After the first blast, we knew instantly we were in big trouble. Everyone scrambled to get inside the house. Kids were screaming, women were crying. We managed to shut the patio doors before it really took hold. The blasts shattered windows, dozens of car alarms were set off, dogs were barking, some poor fucker fell off a shed and broke their leg. The chaos went on for what seemed like ages and then it was all over. We achieved our aim, it was spectacular.

Unfortunately, the police didn't appreciate our display, but we didn't hang around long enough to hear what they had to say. We scarpered, leaving his brother in law to take the rap. He told us later the conversation went something like this.

'I don't know what happened officer they just went off. We even kept them in a box.'

'And where did you purchase these fireworks, sir?'

'Yeah that's it, it's the shops fault. They could have killed us, selling us those dodgy fireworks.' He got off with a slapped wrist.

Random Stuff

You know you're a veteran when:

1. You find yourself saluting random strangers
2. There's no one around, you start marching, swinging your arms shoulder height. Suddenly that umbrella becomes a pace/swagger stick or drum major's mace as you go off marching into the distance whistling Colonel Bogey with a big smile on your face.

3. You refer to the wife as Commanding Officer.
4. You read junk mail catalogues from cover to cover.
5. You find yourself trying to explain what a "doobrieferkin" means to your civvy mates.
6. Your Facebook profile photo is one of you looking cool in a Rambo pose with your SA80 SLR.
7. Trying to explain to your civvy mates that two's up is not a sex position.
8. You hate people who talk bollocks, where the subject matter doesn't come anywhere close to warrant a conversation. (Being bladdered – drunk- is the only exception.)
9. You refuse to use blue pens for anything.
10. You shout 'MEDIC!' or 'MAN DOWN!' at the top of your voice, when your civvy mates fall over shitfaced.
11. You find yourself shouting 'GET OFF THE FUCKING GRASS!' at your grand kids.
12. You get the pub darts team calling the opposition "the enemy."

13. Your doorbell sounds off with, 'halt who goes there', and on the second ring, 'halt hands up, I am ready to fire.'
14. Use either your whole military number, or the last four digits, for nearly every password or pin you have.
15. Anything you can't find is AWOL and everything you notice is SEEN.
16. Your Gran falls over you shout, 'TAKE COVER!'

17. You always use a lighter to remove loose threads.

18. You always get up and follow your buddy when he goes for a shit.
19. Saying 'mount up', to get everyone in the car.
20. You find it completely acceptable to pick your nose while talking to a complete, stranger or member of the opposite sex.
21. You see any food lying around, as meant for sharing.
22. You iron and spray starch your trousers very hard on one side to get that 1979- 80's look.
23. You feel the need to give "advice" to people who

need it, or don't give a shit.
24. You have a garage full of boxes that haven't been unpacked
25. You still have dohbi tags on your shreddies from Belize 78
26. You see more of your family in one year, than in all the years you served
27. Your 3 year old kid has stopped calling any man in uniform their dad or thinks their real dad lives in mum's phone
28. They ask your kids at school where they're from. They say everywhere
29. When you are driving on the motorway checking your spacing and looking for IED's
30. Your wallet is not full of useless cards anymore, white, yellow, green, Soxmix, tropical disease, does your penis look like this etc. Mind you, I have, to admit that one did come in handy.

If you did or still do any of the above, or they apply to members of your family, it's ok, you're not on your own. I bet you feel slightly less mental now!

CHAPTER 13

GOING OUT

Now all you have to do is look out of the window, before you decide what to wear, rather than checking Part I orders or Company Detail to see what someone else says you are allowed to wear. You iron your own clothes, because you never trust your wife or girlfriend to iron them.

You put on your starched shirt, then slip on your trousers with creases that would be classed as an offensive weapon nowadays. You're nearly ready, all that's left to do now is choose which after shave it will be. Will it be your 25, year old, Paco Rabanne, Old Spice, Brut, Tabac or Aramis? Whatever your choice, once you've splashed it on, it instantly takes you back to a golden age.

AFTERSHAVES

Paco Rabanne: This aftershave was created by Francisco "Paco" Rabaneda Cuervo, aka Paco Rabanne and Puig a fragrance company. They began working together in 1968. The aftershave is still available today.

Old Spice: Was originally launched in 1937 as Early American Old Spice for women. The male version Old Spice came onto the market in 1938. Since 2008 it has been known as Classic Scent.

Brut: Produced by Faberge in 1964, it is still available today. It was easily identifiable by its green bottle with a silver medallion. A cheaper version of the original fragrance became available in 1968, labelled as Brut 33. It was sold in plastic bottles and contained 33% of the original fragrance.

Aramis: Launched by Estee Lauder in 1964, it became a popular fragrance. It is named after one of the Three Musketeers. The fragrance is still sold today.

GRAB A GRANNY

Thursday night is "Grab a Granny night," or international army night out. Wherever it may be, you knew you were in for a great night. I remember it like it was yesterday. There you were, out of your tree, supported by the rest of your buddies, all wearing the same aftershave, aggressively staring at the really, good, looking girls, who are way out of your league. Saying things like, 'You see her over there, I've shagged that, and her and her mate! '

Sometime during the evening, when you've moved on to Pernod and blacks and before you get thrown out, it turns into a game of who can get off with the ugliest female. It's game on!

Waking up with a hangover that would kill a civvy, lying next to fattest and ugliest female in town, makes you a legend with your mates. They were some of the best nights ever.

Confucius say: Sex is like the army, the closer you are to discharge, the better you feel.

YOU ARE A LEGEND...

MILITARY MODE

That was back then, now it's... After arriving at the pub five minutes early, you wait for your civvy mates to turn up. Your civvy mates finally arrive. The first thing you do is go back into military mode.

'Get them in then.'

Get them to buy you a beer. You don't care what it's called as long, as someone else has bought it. You sit with your back to the wall, so you can keep an eye on anyone acting suspicious or confrontational, and making sure you've got a clear escape route.

After a few more, free beers, it's game on. You start using target indication to point out the birds, but your civvy mates just want to talk shop, they're not interested. The boring bunch of let downs. The birds aren't interested in you either, especially when you insist on dancing like a twat, Ricky Gervais style.

Back when you were in the military, your mates would have joined in. Not this bunch, they just stand there open mouthed and start walking away in embarrassment.

'I'm not with him!'

It's then, that you start to wonder why they came out with you in the first place. What did the they expect, a game of fucking bingo at the local bingo hall? They're a bunch of boring bastards, who are scared of turning up at work the next day shitfaced and three hours late.

A few more beers and it's time to hit the road, but surely you can't leave a bar that is still open? That's unheard of for any military veteran. For the first time, you break that golden rule and head home. After all, your new civvy mates deserted you ages ago. Your next port of call is the chippy next door. It was just closing until you turned up, they reluctantly serve you.

'Yes sir, what would you like?'
'I'll have a portion of chips, mushy peas, and a baby's head.' They refuse to serve you for some reason.

Ten minutes later, after wandering around the town, you haven't got a clue where you are. Funny that, you might get lost coming home from the pub, but you know the street layout of West Belfast like the back of your hand. You flag down a taxi, half way home, you realise you're flat broke. Doing a runner from a moving taxi without paying won't work without a camp to hide in.

It's four in the morning, you eventually arrive home looking like an extra from the walking dead, well you think it's your home. Why does every house look the same?

Your neighbours don't appreciate you banging on every door in the street, until you get the right one. You're home at last, safe, now you can get that precious two hours sleep, before the missus wakes you up for work. That brings back memories.

INSTITUTIONALISED

Yes, I still have my military traits. Most people who know me, know I'm ex-military, but nothing could have prepared me for what I experienced when I contacted one of my ex-army mates, Jimbo. I hadn't seen him for years. Jimbo, I always remembered was army barmy, he'd done his 22 years. I was interested in finding out how he was coping. He invited me and the missus around for drink. I felt a bit sorry for him after finding out his missus had left him.

I'd never met his missus while I was in the army. I know what her boobs looked like. The same goes for the rest of my squaddie mates, wives and girlfriends. I know what their boobs look like even though I have never met any of them!!

As soon as he opened the door, it was like going back in time. There was Jimbo, dressed in full combats, with his dog tags daggling around his neck. I was starting to have second thoughts already.

After guiding us into his front room, he went off to make us a drink. I couldn't believe my eyes. The wall was covered in framed pictures of Russian military vehicles from the cold war, T72's, T64-65's, BRDM 2's, BMPS and that was just the start.

The whole of the back wall was taken up by a huge monstrosity, pretending to be a wall unit, made from old MFO boxes, he'd left the army with. They were held together using army screws, and laminate-wood-look paper that had been glued on to the surfaces. It even had a built, in bar, containing Ashbach, applecorn, Herforder beer and Jagermister. Another wall was covered in dozens of old, military band music LP covers, featuring Wembley Pageant, Edinburgh Tattoo, the Royal Tournament, to name just a few. But the weirdest thing of all, as we sat down on his camouflage patterned sofa, was the Airfix Lancaster bomber and spitfire models dangling from the ceiling using cotton thread, there was even a thunderbird 2 model.

'Come on, we're going,' the missus said standing up.

Just as she said that, Jimbo appeared with three mugs of tea, NATO standard. We stayed for about an hour, talking about old times, then the subject turned to his missus. It turned out his missus had left him a few years ago, the poor sod. Her, I mean! I asked him what happened. He answered, 'She said she was going to the shop and asked me if I wanted anything. I said yes, get me a Mars bar. I waited and waited. I didn't get the Mars bar and I never saw her again.'

Jimbo had no need to work. He was a right tight bastard in the Army. He saved every penny he earnt. Now, with his full army pension, the only time he goes out of the house, is to the shops every Saturday morning at 10.00 hours without fail.

It was when he wanted to take me up in his loft to show his noddy suits and gas masks ready for the big bang, I knew it was time to leave. My missus later thought he was lying, and his missus could be up there zipped up in a body bag. He did say though, if the inevitable did happen and the bomb did go off, just pop around and he'll sort us out with a couple of noddy suits and gas masks. Bless him, that's army buddies for you, mates till the end. There were no gamma rays or Beta particles on him. Gas... gas... gas...

CHAPTER 14

SENSE OF HUMOUR

When you were in the military you couldn't go a day without hearing some sort of joke, usually a cock joke. The humour can go deeper, much deeper depending on the circumstances. Whether you're Army, Navy or Air force, there is nobody better blessed with a dark sense of humour than a member of the military. It's all about the ability to crack a joke when your backs are against the wall, it's just a way of coping with fear.

Yes, we've all heard the odd sick joke or comment at work, at a party or down the pub, but before the joke comment is told, the teller always looks round to see whose listening, so the teller doesn't upset certain people. The veteran takes the alternative view, he targets those people on purpose. He's after a response.

Funerals are the best places to tell that sort of joke, where everyone is being so respectful and on their best behaviour, but there's always one and it's usually a veteran who likes to take the seriousness away from the situation. Here are a few typical comments, "I know how you feel, my dog died last week," "he looks better dead than he did alive."

The real dark humour will always come out when faced with tragic circumstances. For example, this is a true story. After a road accident, a young man lays in the road, he is clearly dead, missing the right hand, some of his torso, his left arm and his head. A right mess. The copper would say "what a waste." The ambulance man would say "oh, we see this thing every day." But a soldier would say to the paramedic, without thinking, 'hasn't left you and much to work with, has he?'

THE NUMBERS GAME

By 1950, the Army introduced a new number system for all new recruits, commencing with 22000000.

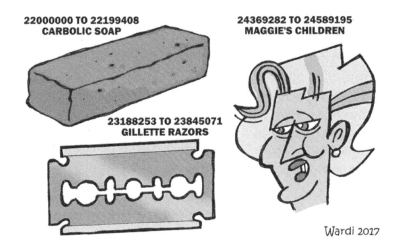

22199409 to 23188252 before October,1955 blanco rash
23845072 to 24057159 before April,1965 The Beatles

24057160 TO 24182226 THE WORLD CUP

Wardi 2017

24182227 to 24369281 before September, 1975 OP Banner
24589196 to 24753060 before end 1985 Paco Rabanne and Aramis
24753061 to ???????? still being issued, comfy helmets, a rifle you can break

Carbolic Soap

Carbolic acid was discovered in 1834, by a German chemist, Friedlieb Ferdinand Runge. Its antiseptic qualities were discovered by Dr Joseph Lister in 1865 at Glasgow Royal Infirmary. The first commercially produced bars of carbolic soap, under the name of lifebuoy, became available in 1894, produced by William Lever.

Blanco

Blanco came into use from 1880. It was used to clean and colour equipment used by soldiers. It

came in several different colours. The introduction of synthetic webbing lead to the demise of Blanco.

Op Banner

Operation Banner was the name given to the British Forces in Northern Ireland from August 1969 to July 2007. The number of serving personnel who died during Op Banner was 1441. MOD documents show 722 were killed by paramilitaries and 719 died from other causes.

MEMORY

Isn't it funny how you can forget the currency exchange rates for all the countries you were posted to, but you can remember the price of a whore back then, right down to the different services they offered... or is that just me?

You use your postings as benchmarks of your life. I was out in Belize when my wife had our first child. I was in the middle of a basketball game against a bunch of matelots. And the wife must have fallen pregnant with our third child when I was on 4 days R&R from Belfast in 82 ...well I hope she did!

I also struggle to change a tyre on my car, but I can remember how to change a track on a 15 ton, APC 20 years later.

OLD VETERAN

My missus says I'm starting to moan constantly about everything nowadays, and I get worse every day. No, I, fucking, don't, but have you seen the price of things in your local charity shops, £3.99 for a pair of slippers? they're having a laugh! what's the country coming to?

Another sure sign you are past it, is when you wake up and all the wrong body parts are stiff.

Instead of sending the 18-year old's off to fight a war, they ought to send us veterans, as long, as you're under 85. Yes, we might be dinosaurs of the finest order, fought the Romans and washed in carbolic soap, with belt lines a couple of inches below our man tits, and balls longer than our dicks. But we can still fight anyone you know.... just as long as we can have a good sit down afterwards!

If we got captured by the enemy, we wouldn't tell them anything. The main reason being, we're that old we wouldn't be able to remember anything, apart from our name, rank, and serial number, that one thing we never forget. Ok, that might be a bit of a challenge for some of us!

Our military days are long gone now, a distant memory. You're a soldier for life, it's just the uniform that changes.

Milan is now a place in Italy, Carl Gustav is not an 84mm anti-tank weapon, but a chef in the local restaurant, and an SLR now means Single Lens Reflex. Enjoy what you've got left, veterans!

Made in the USA
Coppell, TX
11 April 2024